Unlocked Answers

How I Remembered Who I Am

Karen Abbott-Trimuel

ISBN (Paperback): 978-1-7362815-8-1

ISBN (EPUB): 978-1-7362815-9-8

Printed in the United States of America

Life is the whole. Everything else lives inside it. –
KAT

Dedication

This book is dedicated to the quiet voice within each of us that patiently waits for our return.

To my mother, my father, and my brother, whose transitions from this life reminded me that our time here is sacred and that love continues to guide us beyond what we can see.

To my husband, my children, my grandchildren, and my great-grandchild – the living reflections of the legacy we build through love, growth, and remembrance.

To my daughter and my son, who stood beside me in a moment of truth. Your willingness to meet that moment with open hearts reminded me that healing does not belong to one person alone – it belongs to the family willing to grow together. Your acceptance allowed layers to fall away not only in my life, but in ours together. For that, I am deeply thankful.

And to those who will read these words long after I am gone, may this work remind you that the answers you seek have always lived within you.

May we all have the courage to remember who we are – and the grace to forgive the layers we once carried.

Acknowledgements

This journey did not unfold in isolation.

I am deeply thankful for the experiences, challenges, and quiet moments that asked me to look honestly at my life and listen to the voice within me.

To my family, who continue to grow, learn, and evolve alongside me – thank you for the love that reminds me daily that life is meant to be lived in wholeness.

To those who have walked beside me at different points along this journey, offering encouragement, reflection, and truth when it was needed most.

To the readers who will encounter this work now, and in the future – including those generations who may read these pages long after my time here has passed – know that this book is part of a legacy meant to remind you of something simple and powerful:

You do not have to become someone new.

You only need to remember who you are.

Contents

PREFACE

THE QUESTIONS THAT BEGAN THE JOURNEY

Several years ago, I created a workbook titled *Unlocking the Answers to Who I Am*. At the time, I believed I was offering others a collection of thoughtful questions – an opportunity to pause long enough to listen to themselves more honestly. The workbook invited readers to reflect on their lives, their values, their relationships, and the quiet voice that often goes unheard beneath the responsibilities of everyday living. What I did not realize then was that those questions were not only meant for others. They were meant for me to revisit as well. The questions I wrote slowly began asking something of my own life.

Not all at once.

Not in dramatic ways.

But gently, over time.

They began inviting me to sit with myself more honestly than I ever had before.

At first, the process felt uncomfortable. I began noticing places where the life I was living did not fully match the life I felt within myself. I began recognizing roles I had been carrying, expectations I had been meeting, and identities I had been performing without ever truly pausing to ask whether they were mine to carry. The questions that once seemed simple began opening doors within me.

They slowed me down.

They invited reflection.

And little by little, they began revealing something I had not fully recognized before. The journey I thought was about becoming someone new was actually about remembering who I had always been. This book is not a replacement for the workbook. It is what unfolded after living the questions. It is the reflection that emerged after the layers began to fall away. It is the story of how searching slowly gave way to remembering...

and how remembering ultimately led me home.

PROLOGUE

THE QUESTION I COULD NOT ANSWER

Long before I created the workbook *Unlocking the Answers to Who I Am*, there was a moment in my life that quietly planted the seed for everything that followed. At the time, I did not realize how important that moment would become. I was leaving a position with an employer who held a high-level leadership role. When I shared my decision to resign, she did not want me to go. She asked if there was anything that could be done to make me stay. Then she asked a simple question.

"What do you want?"

She meant the question in a practical way. She wanted to know what it would take for me to remain in the position. But when I heard the question, something deeper stirred within me. The words did not land as a workplace conversation. They landed as something much broader.

What do you want?

Not just in this job.

In your life.

In that moment, I realized something that surprised me. I did not have an answer. I could speak about responsibilities. I could describe the roles I carried. I could explain the expectations I was meeting. But when the question became personal – when it became honest – I did not know what I wanted. That realization stayed with me long after that conversation ended. It followed me quietly for months. Then years. Because once a question like that enters your life, it does not easily disappear.

I began noticing how often people move through life without ever pausing to ask themselves what they truly want.

We fulfill responsibilities.

We meet expectations.

We follow paths that seem logical or responsible.

But somewhere along the way, many of us forget to ask ourselves the simplest questions.

What do I want?

The fact that I could not answer that question unsettled me.

Not in a dramatic way.

But in a quiet way that stayed with me.

Eventually, I made a promise to myself. I would search for the answer. And I would never again find myself unable to respond when life asked me that question. That promise became the beginning of something I could not yet see clearly. The search for what I wanted slowly led me to two deeper questions. Questions that would later become the foundation of the workbook I eventually created.

The first question was simple. Who am I?

The second question followed naturally behind it. What makes me happy?

At the time, I did not know that those questions would guide me through years of reflection, stillness, awakening, and remembering. I only knew that the answers mattered. And that I was finally willing to look for them. What I did not understand then was that the questions themselves were already leading me somewhere.

Not forward.

But inward.

And that quiet turning inward would eventually change everything.

A Gentle Reminder

Some questions do not leave us because they are meant to lead us home.
-KAT

CHAPTER ONE

THE LIFE I THOUGHT I WAS SUPPOSED TO LIVE

There came a time in my life when the questions I had written to share with others quietly began asking something of me. Years earlier, I had created a workbook titled *Unlocking the Answers to Who I Am: A Self-Rediscovery Workbook*. At the time, I believed the questions I had written might help others pause long enough to hear themselves clearly. They invited people to reflect on their values, their relationships, their desires, and the quiet voice that often goes unheard beneath the responsibilities of daily life.

Looking back now, I realize the questions did not begin with the workbook. They began years earlier with a conversation I could not forget – when someone once asked me a simple question: "What do you want?" At the time, I did not know how to answer. What I did not realize was that those questions were not only meant for others. They were meant for me as well.

Not rushed.

Not through some loud dramatic moment of awakening.

But slowly and quietly – through small moments that required me to sit with myself in a way I had never done before.

At first there was discomfort. A feeling I could not quite explain, yet a feeling I wanted to quickly escape. From the outside, my life appeared full. I had responsibilities, roles, expectations, and relationships that required my attention. But internally, something felt unfamiliar. Or perhaps more honestly, I felt unfamiliar to myself. It was as if I had been living according to a set of expectations that were never my own.

At the time, I did not yet have the language to describe what I was feeling. I only knew that the questions I had once written for others and thought I had answered – were beginning to echo within me again. And those questions were not asking for quick answers.

They were asking me to be honest.

***

The Day I Asked Who I Really Was

There are moments in life when a question appears quietly and waits patently for your attention. Not because someone asked it out loud, but because something inside of you is seeking an honest answer.

For many years, I moved through life believing I already knew who I was. I had roles. I had responsibilities. I had expectations that shaped the way I showed up in the world. Like most people, I wore the identities that life handed to me.

Daughter.

Partner.

Professional.

Friend.

Provider.

Each role carried its own definition of who I was supposed to be. And for a long time, I honored those roles without questioning them too deeply. I showed up, I performed well, and I did what I believed was expected of me. From the outside, everything appeared steady. But something inside of me was beginning to notice a quiet distance between the life I was living and the person I felt myself to be.

It was not loud.

It did not arrive with disruption or crisis.

It arrived as a question.

Who am I?

At first, the question seemed simple. It felt like something that could be answered quickly if I simply listed the pieces of my life. I could have said:

I am the work I do.

I am the roles I hold.

I am the relationships I maintain.

I am the responsibilities I carry.

But the question did not settle. It remained. And over time I began to realize that the answers I had been giving were not actually answering the question at all. They were describing my life.

Not myself.

There is a difference between describing what we do and recognizing who we are. One can be shaped by expectations. The other must come from within. This realization was subtle, but it changed something in the way I began to see myself. It made me curious in a way I had not been before. Instead of assuming that I already knew who I was, I began to observe myself more carefully.

I noticed when I felt fully aligned with my actions.

I noticed when I felt slightly disconnected from them.

I noticed the moments when my voice felt strong and the moments when it quietly stepped back to make room for others.

And slowly I began to see something that had always been present but rarely acknowledged. The self beneath the roles.

The self that existed before expectations shaped my choices.

The self that did not need permission to exist.

This realization did not arrive quickly. It unfolded slowly through reflection. Through quiet moments and stillness. Through questions that were not trying to produce immediate answers, but instead asking me to listen more carefully to my own life.

Eventually, those reflections became the foundation of the workbook titled *Unlocking the Answers to Who I Am*. What I believed at the time was a guide for others to explore these questions. But what I did not fully understand then was that I was also creating a guide for myself. The workbook was the beginning of a deeper journey. A journey that started with asking "Who am I?" But would eventually lead me somewhere even more meaningful.

Back to myself.

A Moment for the Reader

If you pause for a moment and consider your own life, you may notice something similar. Many of us can easily describe our roles. We can list the responsibilities we carry and the expectations we meet each day. But when the question becomes more honest – when the roles fall away for a moment – another question sometimes appears:

Who am I when the roles are not speaking for me?

That question is not meant to rush you toward an answer. It is meant to open a door.

Author's Reflection: The Beginning of Remembering

Looking back now, I see that the question 'Who am I?" was not asking me to construct a new identity. It was asking me to remember something that had always been there. At the time, I believed I was beginning a journey of becoming. But life would eventually show me something different.

I was not becoming someone new.

I was remembering who I had always been.

And that remembering began with a single, honest question. Who am I – beneath the roles, the expectations, and the life I had learned to perform?

CHAPTER TWO

THE LIFE I COULD NO LONGER IGNORE

Long before I began asking the question "Who am I?", there was a version of me who never needed to ask it. That version existed naturally.

Children rarely question who they are. They move through the world with a kind of honesty that has not yet learned how to perform. They speak when they feel something. They laugh when joy appears. They follow curiosity without asking permission.

There is a quiet freedom in that stage of life. Not because children know everything about themselves, but because they have not yet learned to doubt their own presence. When I began reflecting on my life more deeply, I realized something important. There was a time when I already knew myself. Not in a way that could be explained through titles or accomplishments, but in the way a person simply knows how to be. That younger version of me was curious.

She noticed things.

She listened.

She felt deeply connected to the world around her and within her.

She did not yet carry the weight of expectations. But life, as it does for all of us, slowly introduced new influences.

School.

Family expectations.

Social roles.

Ideas about success.

Ideas about what it meant to be good, responsible, and worthy.

None of these things are inherently wrong. Many of them are part of learning how to move through the world with others. But somewhere along the way, something subtle began to happen. The natural voice that once moved freely began learning when to pause. When to adjust. When to make room for what others expected.

This is something many of us experience without realizing it. We learn how to behave in ways that help us to belong. We learn how to meet expectations. We learn how to shape ourselves so the world around us feels comfortable with who we are. And slowly, almost without noticing, we begin to live slightly outside of ourselves. Not completely disconnected. But slightly removed from the quiet center that once felt so natural.

For many years, I did not recognize this shift. Life continued moving forward. Responsibilities grew. Roles expanded. And the younger version of myself slowly became a distant memory rather than an active presence. But when I began asking deeper questions about my life, something interesting happened. That younger voice had never disappeared.

It had simply been waiting.

Quietly waiting beneath the layers of expectations and responsibilities that life had placed around it. Meeting that younger version of myself again was not about returning to childhood. It was about recognizing that the core of who I had always been was still present.

Still observing.

Still guiding.

Still quietly offering truth when I became willing to listen.

That realization was powerful because it changed how I viewed the journey of remembering myself. I had once believed that discovering myself meant creating something new. But remembering my younger self revealed something different. I did not need to create a new identity.

I needed to remove the layers that had slowly formed around the one that was already there.

A Moment for the Reader

If you pause for a moment and think about your own younger self, you may notice something familiar. There was likely a time when certain things came naturally to you. Ways of expressing yourself. Interests that made you feel alive. A way of seeing the world that felt honest and clear.

Over time, some of those things may have been encouraged. Others may have been quietly set aside in order to fit into expectations. But often, the parts of ourselves that felt most natural early in life never truly disappear. They wait.

Sometimes quietly.

Sometimes patiently.

Until we are ready to meet them again.

***

Author's Reflection: The Return Begins

Meeting my younger self again did not happen all at once. It unfolded through reflection and stillness. Through noticing what felt authentic and what felt shaped by expectation. Through slowly trusting the quiet inner voice that had been present all along.

At the time, I thought I was simply rediscovering parts of myself that had been forgotten. But now I understand something deeper. Those parts were never lost. They were simply waiting for me to remember them.

CHAPTER THREE

LOOKING IN THE MIRROR

For years, I believed clarity would arrive quickly. I thought there would be a moment when everything would suddenly make sense – when the answers would appear clearly and the path forward would reveal itself without uncertainty. But life rarely unfolds that way. Instead, my journey toward listening and returning to myself unfolded slowly. It happened through cycles. Cycles that often began with life presenting a challenge I did not fully understand at the time.

Sometimes those challenges appeared through relationships.

Sometimes through work.

Sometimes through moments when the life I was living no longer felt aligned with who I felt myself to be inside.

When those moments arrived, they often brought discomfort. Questions appeared again. The same ones I thought I had already answered.

Why does this feel wrong?

Why do I feel disconnected from something that once seemed certain?

Why am I ignoring the quiet voice inside me?

At first, I did what many people do.

I continued moving forward.

I kept working.

I kept fulfilling responsibilities.

I kept convincing myself that if I stayed busy enough, the discomfort would eventually disappear. But life has a way of asking us to slow down. Eventually, the challenges led me into stillness. Not the kind of stillness we plan for ourselves, but the kind that appears when we realize that continuing in the same way is no longer possible.

In those quiet moments of stillness, something began to shift. Without the constant movement of daily responsibilities, I began to hear something that had always been there. My own voice.

Not the voice shaped by expectations.

Not the voice responding to what others needed from me.

But the quiet internal voice that had patiently waited for my attention.

It did not shout.

It did not demand.

It simply spoke gently... and then patiently waited.

At first, I did not fully trust it. Years of living according to external expectations had taught me to listen outwardly before listening inwardly. But something about the voice felt familiar.

Not new.

Simply... remembered.

Over time I began to notice something about the way life was unfolding. The challenges that brought me to stillness were not random. They were invitations. Each cycle was of-fering the same opportunity:

Pause.

Listen.

Adjust.

At first, I did not always accept the invitation immediate-ly. Sometimes the same lesson returned more than once. Sometimes I repeated patterns before recognizing them. But each time I slowed down long enough to listen honestly and the inner voice became clearer.

Not louder.

Clearer.

Because clarity does not always come from hearing more noise. Sometimes clarity comes from finally removing the noise that was already there. With each cycle, something subtle began to change.

I trusted myself more.

I questioned expectations more carefully.

I noticed when my actions aligned with the voice within me... and when they did not.

And slowly, almost without realizing it, I began living dif-ferently. I was finally listening to the part of myself that had always known. Looking back now, I can see that those cycles were not interruptions in my life. They were the process of awakening.

Each challenge led me to stillness.

Each moment of stillness opened space for reflection.

Each reflection brought a little more awareness.

And that awareness slowly became remembering.

A Moment for the Reader

If you think about your own life, you may notice similar cycles.

Moments when something felt misaligned.

Moments when life slowed you down long enough to notice it.

Moments when a quiet internal voice suggested a different way forward.

Many of us hear that voice. The difference is whether we allow ourselves to listen. Listening inwardly is not something we learn all at once. It is something we practice each time life invites us to pause.

***

Author's Reflection: The Awakening Begins

At the time, I thought I was simply learning to make better decisions. But something deeper was happening. The cycles of challenge, stillness, and reflection were slowly guiding me toward something I had not fully named yet.

Awakening.

Not the kind that announces itself loudly. The kind that unfolds quietly through honest listening. And that awakening would eventually lead me to something even more meaningful:

Remembering.

CHAPTER FOUR

SITTING WITH MYSELF

There was a time when someone could have asked me one simple question: What do you want? And I would have been quick to give an answer. Like many people, I had goals. I had ideas about success. I had expectations regarding the direction my life should move and what it should look like when I arrived. But something interesting began to happen when I started reflecting more honestly on my life. The answers I once provided were not as clear as they once seemed to be. When I looked closely, I began to realize something I had not noticed before. Many of the things I believed I wanted were not truly my own. They were shaped by what I had been taught to value. They were influenced by what the world around me defined as success.

They reflected expectations that had been quietly handed to me over time.

Work hard.

Achieve more.

Prove your worth.

Build a life that others admire.

None of these ideas are inherently wrong. But when I began asking myself the question, "What do I truly want?", something inside of me hesitated. Not because I did not care about my life. But because I realized I had never fully separated my desires from the expectations that surrounded them.

For a while, the question remained unanswered. And that was uncomfortable. We often believe that clarity means having immediate answers. But sometimes clarity begins when we realize the answers we had been giving are not entirely honest. At first, I could not define what I wanted.

Not clearly.

Not honestly.

Because the life I had been building had been shaped by ideas that were not fully mine.

Life continued unfolding, and the cycles that had led me to stillness and reflection began revealing something deeper. As the layers of expectation slowly faded, I began to notice what had been missing.

It was not achievement.

It was not recognition.

It was something I had not known to look for.

Peace.

Alignment.

Wholeness.

These were not things I had originally thought to pursue. They were not the goals I had written down when thinking about success. But once I recognized them, I could not ignore how important they were.

Peace was the feeling of no longer needing to perform in order to belong. Alignment was the experience of living in a way that matched the truth I felt within myself. Wholeness was the understanding that nothing about me needed to be hidden, reshaped, or diminished in order to be accepted.

These realizations did not appear overnight. They emerged gradually as I continued listening to myself more honestly. Each layer that faded revealed something clearer. What I truly wanted was not the life I had been taught to chase. What I truly wanted was the freedom to live in alignment with who I already was. And once I recognized that, everything began to shift.

Not all at once.

But steadily.

When peace, alignment, and wholeness become the foundation of your choices, the direction of your life begins to shift naturally.

Looking back now, I understand something that I could not see clearly before. The life I thought I was searching for was not something I needed to build from the outside. It was something I needed to uncover from within.

A Moment for the Reader

If someone asked you today, "What do you want?", Would you answer quickly? Or would you pause long enough to separate your voice from the expectations around you?

If you were to pause, you might discover something deeper. Sometimes the life we are trying to build is not actually the life we want. Sometimes the life we want is much simpler.

More peaceful.

More aligned.

More whole.

But recognizing that requires honesty with ourselves. And honesty often begins when we are willing to let the layers fall away.

***

Author's Reflection: A Shift Toward Alignment

As I began recognizing what I truly wanted, something else started to change. The way I viewed my relationships. Because when you begin aligning with yourself, the way you connect with others also begins to shift. And that realization would lead me into the next part of my journey. Understanding how relationships reflect the alignment we carry within ourselves.

CHAPTER FIVE

THE VOICE THAT WAS WAITING

As I continued learning to listen to myself and recognize what I truly wanted, another part of my life began to reveal something important.

My relationships.

Relationships are often where we see ourselves most clearly, even when we are not looking for that reflection.

For many years, I believed that maintaining harmony in relationships meant adjusting myself when necessary. I believed that making space for others was simply part of being loving, supportive, and responsible.

And in many ways, it is.

Relationships require care. They require understanding. They require a willingness to consider another person's perspective. But somewhere along the way, I began to notice something subtle.

Sometimes I was not simply making space for others.

Sometimes I was moving myself out of the space entirely.

There were moments when I would silence my voice so that someone else would feel more comfortable. Moments when I would adjust my needs so that another person would not feel challenged or inconvenienced. Moments when I would say yes even when something inside of me was quietly asking for a pause.

At first, these choices seemed small. Even generous. But over time, I began to see a pattern. In certain relationships, I had slowly learned to make myself uncomfortable so that others could feel comfortable. And when that happens repeatedly, something important begins to change.

Not only in the relationship.

But within ourselves.

Because every time we silence our own alignment in order to maintain connection, we move slightly further away from the center of who we are.

What made this realization difficult at first was that my intentions had never been harmful.

I was trying to maintain peace.

I was trying to care for the people around me.

I was trying to be understanding.

But understanding others should never require abandoning ourselves. This was one of the most important lessons I had to learn. Healthy relationships do not require us to disappear. They require us to remain present.

Present with our voice.

Present with our boundaries.

Present with our alignment.

When I began recognizing this, something else became clear. The discomfort I had sometimes felt in certain relationships was not always about the other person. It was about the distance between my external actions and my internal truth. When those two things are not aligned, something inside of us notices. And that inner voice quietly reminds us that something needs attention.

As I continued learning to listen to myself more honestly, I began making small adjustments.

I allowed myself to speak more clearly.

I allowed myself to pause before agreeing to things that did not feel aligned.

I allowed myself to consider my own well-being alongside the needs of others.

These were not dramatic changes. They were quiet shifts in the way I chose to live. But those quiet shifts began changing the quality of my relationships. Some connections became stronger because honesty created deeper understanding. Some connections naturally loosened because they had relied on a version of me that was no longer present.

At first, that felt uncertain. But over time, something beautiful became clear. The relationships that remained were not built on performance. They were built on authenticity. And when two people are able to meet each other from a place of authenticity, something powerful happens.

Connection becomes lighter.

More honest.

More peaceful.

Because neither person is carrying the weight of pretending.

Looking back now, I understand that relationships were never meant to require self-abandonment. They were meant to reflect the alignment we carry within ourselves. And as my alignment grew stronger, the reflections around me began to change as well.

A Moment for the Reader

If you think about your own relationships, you may notice moments when you adjusted yourself in order to maintain harmony. Sometimes those adjustments are healthy. But sometimes they quietly ask more of us than we realize.

If you paused long enough to listen to your own alignment, you might ask yourself a simple question: Where in my life have I been making myself uncomfortable so that others can feel comfortable?

The answer to that question is not meant to create blame or regret. It is meant to open the door to honesty. And honesty is where authentic relationships begin.

***

Author's Reflection: Alignment Changes Everything

As I continued aligning with myself, I noticed something else changing. The way I showed up in my own life. The more I honored my internal voice, the less I felt the need to perform for the world around me. And slowly, the identity I had once carried began to soften. The roles were still there. But they were no longer defining me.

Something deeper was beginning to emerge. The authentic self that had always existed beneath the layers.

CHAPTER SIX

WHEN THE MASK BEGIN TO DISSOLVE

There came a time in my life when something inside of me became very uncomfortable. Not physically uncomfortable. But internally unsettled. It was a feeling I could not easily explain at first. I began to feel like an imposter in my own life. From the outside, things may have looked normal.

Roles were being fulfilled.

Responsibilities were being handled.

But inside, something felt misaligned.

When I looked at my life honestly, I realized something difficult. I did not recognize myself. That realization did not come with clarity or peace. It came with discomfort. Once you recognize that you no longer recognize yourself, a deeper question follows.

How did I get here?

At first, I thought the discomfort meant something outside of me needed to change. But as I began sitting with myself honestly, I realized something personal. I had not been protecting myself.

Not emotionally.

Not spiritually.

Not energetically.

Instead, I had been constantly adapting. Fulfilling roles and meeting expectations.

Performing versions of myself that were acceptable to the environments around me. And the longer I lived that way, the further I moved from the center of who I actually was. The roles and expectations did not dissolve immediately. That came later.

First came something much more confronting. I had to sit with myself.

Still.

Honest.

Uncomfortable.

This is the part of the journey many people avoid. Because sitting with yourself means facing the parts of your life that no longer feel true. It means acknowledging the mask. And acknowledging the mask means acknowledging the ways you have participated in maintaining it. This was the beginning of my shadow work.

I had to look in the mirror and see clearly what I had been avoiding.

Not with shame.

But with honesty.

And during that time, something else began to happen. The internal voice I had once ignored began to speak again.

Quietly at first.

But unmistakably.

And when I heard it clearly, something surprising happened.

It did not feel angry.

It felt disappointed.

Not disappointed in a condemning way, but in the way someone feels when they know you are capable of more than what you are allowing yourself to live. That internal voice was not criticizing me. It was calling me. It was asking me to return. Because something inside of me knew there were greater experiences ahead.

More aligned ways of living.

More honest ways of being.

And the voice was reminding me that I was wasting time pretending to be someone I was not. I felt that message deeply. So, I did something I had not done in a long time. I became still.

Not temporarily still.

Intentionally still.

I stopped chasing.

I stopped performing.

I stopped trying to maintain identities that no longer felt honest.

And in that stillness, something remarkable began to happen. The mask did not need to be ripped away. It began dissolving on its own. Because once you stop performing for the world around you, the mask no longer has a reason to exist. The roles I had carried did not disappear. But they stopped defining me. Something deeper began emerging. My core – the self that had always been there. The self that had existed long before the expectations.

Long before the performances.

Long before the mask.

Looking back now, I understand something important. The mask did not disappear because I fought against it. It disappeared because I finally listened to myself.

Once you begin living from your core instead of your mask, something changes permanently. You no longer feel the need to perform for acceptance. Because you have returned to the place where acceptance begins. Within yourself.

A Moment for the Reader

There are moments in life when something inside of us becomes uncomfortable. We may try to ignore it. We may try to distract ourselves from it. But that discomfort often carries an important message. Sometimes it is simply asking us to pause long enough to ask ourselves a question.

Do I recognize the life I am living?

If the answer to that question is uncertain, it may not be a problem. It may be an invitation. An invitation to sit with yourself long enough to hear the voice that has been waiting patiently for your attention.

***

Author's Reflection: The Beginning of Innerstanding

When the noise around me quieted and I began listening to myself more honestly, something deeper began to unfold. I started understanding life differently.

Not just intellectually.

But internally.

What I began experiencing was something I would later describe as innerstanding. A form of knowing that does not come from external instruction. But from alignment within. And that realization would open the next part of the journey.

CHAPTER SEVEN

RECOGNITION

After the mask began dissolving and I allowed myself to become still, something new began to unfold within me. It did not happen suddenly. There was no single moment where everything became clear. Instead, it happened gently.

Quietly.

Over time.

As I continued sitting with myself, listening to my internal voice, and aligning my actions with what I felt internally, something deeper began to take shape. I began to experience life differently. Not just through thought. But through a deeper form of knowing. A knowing that did not come from external instruction. A knowing that came from within.

This is what I later came to call innerstanding. Most of our lives are built around understanding.

Understanding information.

Understanding expectations.

Understanding what others believe to be true.

Understanding often begins externally.

We learn.

We observe.

We interpret.

And those forms of learning are valuable. But innerstanding is different. Innerstanding does not begin with information. It begins with alignment. As my heart softened and my mind, body, and spirit began to move into alignment, something inside of me became clearer. Truth no longer felt like something I needed to search for outside of myself. It began revealing itself within me.

Not loudly.

But steadily.

Innerstanding does not replace understanding. It deepens it. Understanding helps us communicate with the world around us. Innerstanding helps us remain connected to ourselves.

Understanding helps us explain.

Innerstanding helps us recognize.

And recognition changes the way you move through life. When something is truly innerstood, you no longer need constant reassurance from the outside world. You begin trusting the quiet guidance that rises from within.

This kind of knowing grows slowly. It grows through reflection.

Through stillness.

Through honest self-observation.

Through listening more than reacting to the world around you.

As my innerstanding deepened, something else began to change. I no longer felt the need to force clarity. I no longer felt pressured to rush toward answers. I began allowing life to reveal itself at its natural pace. And when you begin living this way, something interesting happens. The world around you begins reflecting the alignment you carry within yourself.

Opportunities feel more natural.

Decisions feel less forced.

Relationships become more honest.

Because you are no longer navigating life from confusion. You are navigating life from connection with yourself.

Looking back now, I understand something that once seemed difficult to explain. Innerstanding is not something we acquire. It is something we return to. It is the quiet wisdom that begins revealing itself when we slow down enough to hear it.

A Moment for the Reader

There are moments in life when we search for answers everywhere around us.

Books.

Advice.

External guidance.

And those things can be helpful. But sometimes the clarity we are searching for is already present within us.

Waiting.

Patiently.

If you were to pause long enough to listen to yourself honestly, you might discover something unexpected. You may already know more than you think. Not because someone told you. But because something inside of you recognizes what is true. That recognition is the beginning of innerstanding.

Author's Reflection: When Life Begins to Reflect You Back

As my innerstanding deepened, something remarkable began to happen. The world around me started reflecting what I had discovered within myself.

Situations that once felt confusing began making sense.

Decisions that once felt complicated became simpler.

Life itself began responding differently.

Not because the world had changed. But because I had. And that realization would lead me into the next part of my journey.

RETURNING HOME TO MYSELF

As my innerstanding deepened and I began living more honestly from my core, something unexpected began happening around me. Life started reflecting that alignment back to me.

At first, the changes were subtle.

Nothing dramatic.

Nothing sudden.

But slowly, I began noticing that things felt different. Decisions that once felt heavy began to feel lighter. Situations that once required force began unfolding more naturally. The effort I had once used to push life forward began to soften. And in its place, something else appeared.

Flow.

When you begin living from alignment, life does not necessarily become perfect.

Challenges still exist.

Responsibilities still exist.

But the way you move through them changes. Instead of constantly resisting life, you begin cooperating with it. Instead of forcing outcomes, you begin recognizing direction. And when that happens, life begins reflecting something back to you.

Your own alignment.

One of the first places I noticed this change was in my direction. The opportunities that began appearing no longer felt random. They felt connected. As if life itself was responding to the clarity that had grown within me.

The next change appeared in my relationships. The connections that remained in my life began to feel lighter and more honest. I no longer felt the need to perform or adjust myself in order to belong. The relationships that continued were the ones that could exist alongside my authenticity. And when relationships are built on authenticity, something beautiful happens.

Connection becomes peaceful instead of exhausting.

The most noticeable change appeared within myself. A sense of peace began settling into my life. Not the kind of peace that depends on everything going perfectly. But a deeper peace. A peace that comes from knowing you are no longer abandoning yourself.

I no longer felt like an imposter in my own life.

I no longer felt the pressure to constantly prove who I was. I was simply present.

Present in my decisions.

Present in my relationships.

Present in the direction my life was unfolding.

Looking back now, I understand something clearly. Life had not suddenly changed.

I had.

And when you change the way you show up in your life, life begins responding differently. Because alignment has a way of shaping the experiences that follow it. The more honestly you live, the more honestly life begins meeting you.

A Moment for the Reader

Sometimes we spend years trying to control the direction of our lives.

Trying to force clarity.

Trying to push outcomes.

Trying to prove that we are capable of building the life we want.

But occasionally, something shifts. Instead of forcing life forward, we begin aligning ourselves with what feels honest. And when that happens, life begins reflecting something back to us.

Not perfection.

But direction.

Not certainty.

But peace.

And often, that is enough to remind us that we are finally moving in the right direction.

Author's Reflection: *The Journey of Returning*

As life continued reflecting my alignment back to me, one final realization slowly emerged. The journey I believed I was on – the journey of becoming someone new – had never really been about becoming. It had always been about returning. Returning to the self that existed before the layers.

Before the expectations.

Before the mask.

And when that realization fully settled within me, something very simple became clear.
I had remembered... Who I Am.

CHAPTER NINE

WHEN THE CROWN FOUND ME

I was always finding myself on a journey of becoming.

Becoming stronger.

Becoming wiser.

Becoming more aligned.

Becoming who I was supposed to be.

This is a path that many of us find ourselves on. We believe the purpose of the journey is to build ourselves into something better. To grow into someone new. To transform into a version of ourselves that is more complete.

As my own journey unfolded, something very different revealed itself. My journey was never meant to be one of becoming. I was being guided to remember. And remembering would eventually lead me to returning. That return did not arrive with fanfare.

There were no bells.

No whistles.

No dramatic moment where everything suddenly changed.

Instead, it arrived quietly.

Gently.

Like something that had been waiting patiently for me to notice it. One day, I simply recognized that I felt present in my own life.

Not performing.

Not explaining.

Not chasing validation or reassurance.

Just present.

The searching that once filled my mind had grown quiet. The pressure to prove myself had faded. The need to constantly define who I was had dissolved. Nothing dramatic had happened on the outside. But internally, something had settled. I had returned to myself. The self that existed before the layers.

Before the expectations.

Before the mask.

Before the belief that I had to become something different in order to be enough.

Looking back now, I understand that the journey was never about building a new identity. It was about removing what never truly belonged to me.

Every role.

Every expectation.

Every mask I carried had once served a purpose. They protected me. They helped me navigate environments that required adaptation. They helped me survive seasons when I had not yet learned to trust myself. And for that, I am thankful. But eventually, protection must give way to truth. And truth makes space for return.

Now, when I look at my life, I do not feel the need to explain who I am. I do not feel the need to prove anything to anyone. I feel something much simpler.

Perfection.

Wholeness.

Not perfection in the way the world often describes it. But perfection in motion. The quiet alignment of mind, body, and spirit. The courage to live without an audience. The strength to exist without performance. The return of unconditional love for self.

And perhaps the most beautiful realization of all is this: I was never lost. I was simply waiting for myself to come home.

A Moment for the Reader

There may come a time in your life when you realize something surprising. The person you have been trying to become is not someone new. It is the person you were before the layers were added.

Before expectations shaped your direction.

Before you learned to adjust yourself in order to belong.

When that realization arrives, it may not feel dramatic. It may arrive quietly. Like a deep breath you did not know you were holding. And in that moment, you may recognize something very simple.

You were never lost.

You were remembering.

And remembering is the path that leads us home.

***

Author's Reflection: The Home Within Me

Looking back now, I can see something that once felt difficult to understand. The journey I believed I was on was never asking me to build a new version of myself. It was asking me to release the layers that had slowly formed around the person I had always been.

Every question I asked...

Every moment of stillness...

Every challenge that led me inward...

Was guiding me back to something simple.

Myself.

Not the version shaped by expectation. Not the version performing for acceptance. But the self that existed before the layers were added. And once that realization settled within me, I understood something clearly.

Home was never somewhere I had to travel to.

Home was always within me.

CHAPTER TEN

THE AWAKENING AFTER STILLNESS

Looking back now, I can see that the woman I eventually returned to did not appear suddenly. She was being uncovered slowly through the seasons of my life.

One of those seasons unfolded when I created an event called *Women Are Rising & Unmasking Their Stories*.

At the time, I believed I was simply creating a space where women could tell their stories honestly. We gathered together and listened to the testimonies of women who had experienced trauma and learned to transform it into strength. Their stories were powerful, and the room was often filled with the kind of silence that comes when truth is spoken openly.

I was not originally planning to share my own story. But my daughter insisted that I should. She saw something in me that I had not yet fully seen in myself. And because of her insistence, I told my truth.

Something shifted in that moment.

Speaking my story out loud did not feel like performance. It felt like exposure. Like opening a door that had been closed for many years. And in that moment, something inside of me began to break open.

Not dramatically.

But honestly.

The mask did not fall away all at once, but it began to crack. Layer by layer, pieces of the life I had carefully held together began revealing themselves. I could feel my power returning.

Not quickly.

Not loudly.

But steadily.

I booked a photoshoot for one of the gatherings, and something unexpected happened. Before the photoshoot began, the photographer scheduled a short interview with me. She wanted to learn more about the work we were doing and the purpose behind the gathering.

During the conversation, she asked me a question. As I responded, words came through me that I had not planned to say. I heard myself answer,

"You don't have to look for the crown. You are the crown."

The moment passed, and we continued with the photoshoot. Later, the photographer shared the finished image with me. On the canvas of the photograph, she had placed those very words beside my portrait. I paused when I saw them. I did not remember saying them. So, I went back and watched the recording. And when I heard myself speak those words, something inside of me paused.

For the first time, I recognized a voice that had always lived within me. It was my voice.

Not the voice shaped by expectation.

Not the voice trying to please the room.

But the voice that had been waiting patiently for me to hear it.

From that moment forward, the work began to expand. What started as an event eventually became a community. We created a group called *Women All Rise*, and every month we gathered together. We spoke about the wholeness of life, about boundaries, about self-love, about healing.

Over the years we shared retreats, celebrations, and countless conversations. Many lives were touched. Including my own. At the time, I believed I was leading from strength. And in many ways, I was. But during those years, I also learned something difficult about myself. I was leaking my energy.

Without realizing it, I was making myself uncomfortable in order to keep others comfortable.

Mentally.

Emotionally.

Physically.

Even financially.

People had expectations of me. And for a long time, I tried to meet those expectations. Until the day my inner voice spoke clearly.

During the final retreat, something within me became very clear. As I sat quietly, I recognized that the season I had devoted to pouring into others was coming to completion. The work we had done together had been meaningful, and I felt deep appreciation for the women who had shared that journey with me.

What I did not fully understand then was that the work I had done with those women had also been quietly preparing me for my own return. My inner voice was gently reminding me that it was time to turn my energy inward for a while.

When I returned home from that retreat, I began to see things differently. In the remaining gatherings, I could feel the shift clearly. The season had come to completion. The work we had done together had served its purpose. And now it was time for something else. It was time for me to turn the energy inward.

Closing that chapter of my life was not painful. It felt complete. And once it ended, a different season began.

Stillness.

A Moment for the Reader

There may come a time in your life when something you once built with love reaches its natural completion.

It may have helped many people.

It may have changed lives.

But deep within you, a quiet voice begins to say that the season has ended.

That voice does not mean the work was wrong. It simply means the work is finished. Sometimes the greatest act of courage is recognizing when something beautiful has run its course and allowing yourself to return inward.

Author's Reflection: *Some Seasons Come to a Close*

When I look back at that season now, I feel nothing but appreciation. Those years helped many women find their voices. But they also helped me find mine.

The woman who stood before those rooms of women was not just leading others. She was slowly being led back to herself. And once that return began, something new was waiting for me.

Stillness.

CHAPTER ELEVEN

THE JOURNEY OF REMEMBERING

When the gatherings ended and the rooms grew quiet, my life entered a season I did not fully understand at first.

Everything that once filled my calendar disappeared.

People.

Places.

Responsibilities.

Conversations.

It felt like death. Not physical death, but the end of everything I had once known.

For a while, I felt as though I had disappeared from the life I once lived. There was a kind of nakedness in that season. Without the roles I had carried for so long, I could no longer hide behind them.

I had nothing left to perform.

Nothing left to maintain.

Nothing left to prove.

At first, that kind of exposure felt unfamiliar. But slowly something else began to happen. The nakedness was replaced with something gentler. It felt as though I was being clothed in new fabrics.

Soft fabrics.

Vibrant fabrics.

Smooth and nourishing fabrics that wrapped around the life I was beginning to live.

In that quiet season, something inside of me awakened. Not in a dramatic way. But in a way that made me more aware.

More alert.

More honest with myself.

For the first time in my life, I began considering myself before others. That realization may sound simple. But it changed everything. When I aligned my choices with what was truly for me, I noticed something surprising. Things began to fall into place. Not because I forced them. But because they were already meant for me.

My confidence began to grow. Not the loud kind that demands attention. But the quiet confidence that comes from living honestly.

Authenticity replaced performance.

Boundaries replaced exhaustion.

And the voice that had once whispered began guiding my life more clearly.

It was during this season that my work as a clarity coach began to deepen. Helping others navigate life transitions was no longer something I was trying to do. It was something I had lived. And when you live something deeply enough, your voice naturally carries it.

Looking back now, I understand something that once felt mysterious. Everything that happened before that season was preparing me. The layers I once carried were not mistakes. They were teachers. They guided me to the parts of myself that had been waiting patiently all along.

When the layers finally fell away, what remained was the person I had always been. And that moment felt like a reset.

A return to my original settings.

Not a new life. But the life that was waiting beneath everything I once believed I had to become. Now I move through the world differently.

Not explaining.

Not performing.

Just living.

And allowing my life to reflect the truth I have remembered.

A Moment for the Reader

If life ever brings you to a moment where the roles you once carried begin to fall away, do not rush to replace them. Allow the quiet to do its work. Sometimes the absence of noise is where your true voice finally becomes clear. And when that voice begins guiding your life, you may discover something beautiful.

You are not becoming someone new.

You are simply returning to who you were before the layers were added.

Author's Reflection: The Journey of Remembering

When I look at my life today, I no longer see a journey of becoming. I see a journey of remembering. The questions I once asked slowly unfolded the answers that led me home. And the woman I was searching for was never somewhere ahead of me. She was waiting patiently beneath the layers for my return home.

Chapter Twelve

The Arrival

By the time the questions had led me home, and the layers had fallen away, something quietly settled within me. It was not the kind of arrival that announces itself with celebration or recognition. It was quieter than that. It felt like coming to rest inside my own life.

For much of my journey, I believed that returning to myself would feel dramatic – as if something extraordinary would suddenly appear. But what I discovered instead was something far more meaningful.

Life became lighter.

The weight I once carried – the pressure to perform, to persuade, to prove – slowly dissolved. In its place came a different way of living. A way of living that begins with one simple practice:

Considering myself.

For many years I believed that considering myself meant placing my needs above others. I worried it might look selfish or disconnected from the people around me. But the truth I discovered was very different.

Considering myself means honoring the alignment of my mind, body, and spirit. It means listening carefully to what my life is asking of me. It means activating my discernment and weighing each decision against the boundaries that have been set. And when something does not align with that internal knowing, I allow myself the freedom to pause, reconsider, or step away. This practice changed everything. Because when I began considering myself honestly, I noticed something surprising. Life began responding differently.

Situations that once felt complicated became clear.

Decisions that once required struggle became natural.

The energy I once spent trying to manage everything around me returned to its rightful place within me.

What I came to innerstand is that wholeness is not something we achieve once and then keep forever. Wholeness is something we live. It is the daily alignment of mind, body, and spirit. And when one of those parts moves out of alignment, I feel it immediately.

I notice it.

I listen.

And I return.

Because true peace lives in that alignment.

Not in perfection.

Not in control.

But in the quiet harmony that comes when our inner life and our outer life are no longer separate. This is what surprised me the most after returning to myself.

How light life could feel.

The responsibilities of life did not disappear. The world did not suddenly become easier. But I was no longer carrying layers that were never mine to hold. I was simply living.

Living from the self I had remembered.

Living with the innerstanding that the journey was never about becoming someone new.

It was about uncovering the person who had always been there. The woman I once searched for was not waiting somewhere ahead of me. She was waiting beneath the layers. And when the layers fell away, what remained was wholeness. Not perfection as the world defines it. But the steady alignment of mind, body, and spirit. And in that alignment, something beautiful becomes possible.

Life and the way we live it become one.

There is no separation.

There is only presence.

A Moment for the Reader

If you have walked alongside these pages and recognized parts of yourself along the way, pause here for a moment.

Notice the places in your life where alignment already exists.

Notice the places where your inner voice may be asking for your attention.

And most importantly, allow yourself the freedom to consider yourself. Not from a place of separation from others, but from a place of wholeness within yourself. Because when you live from that place, your life begins to move with a different kind of clarity.

One that does not require force.

One that does not require performance.

Only honesty.

Author's Reflection: The Questions Led Me Home

When I look back over this journey now, I innerstand something that once felt impossible to see clearly. The questions I asked were never meant to lead me somewhere new. They were meant to lead me home. And when I arrived, I discovered something simple and profound. Nothing about me had ever been missing. The self I was searching for had always been there.

Waiting beneath the layers.

Waiting for the moment when I would pause long enough to remember.

I was never lost.

I was simply waiting to remember and return.

EPILOGUE

THE JOURNEY CONTINUES

When I look back over the path that led me here, I see something now that I could not see while I was walking it.

Every question had a purpose.

Every season carried its own lesson.

Even the moments that once felt uncertain were quietly guiding me toward something meaningful.

For many years, I believed I was searching for answers somewhere outside of myself. I believed the next step would reveal them. Or the next experience. Or the next season of life. But the deeper truth revealed itself slowly.

The answers were never waiting somewhere ahead of me. They were waiting within me. Waiting for the moment when I would slow down long enough to listen.

Looking back now, I innerstand something that once seemed difficult to recognize. The journey was never about becoming someone new. It was about returning.

Returning to the self that existed before the layers.

Before the expectations.

Before the roles that slowly shaped the life I thought I was supposed to live.

And when the return finally settled within me, something else became clear. Nothing about me had ever been missing. The strength I once believed I needed to develop was already there. The wisdom I believed I had to acquire had been quietly growing through every experience I lived. Even the parts of my life that once felt confusing had played their role in shaping the person I was becoming aware of.

Today, my life feels lighter than it once did. Not because life has become easier, but because I am no longer carrying layers that were never mine to hold. I live now with a quiet awareness of something simple. Wholeness is not something we achieve once and then keep forever. Wholeness is something we practice. It lives in the alignment of mind, body, and spirit. When one moves out of balance, the others gently ask for attention. And when they move together again, life begins to feel whole. This is the way I live now.

Not perfectly.

But honestly.

And with deep appreciation for the journey that led me home.

If you have walked alongside these pages and recognized parts of your own life within them, I hope you allow yourself the same patience that this journey required of me.

Some questions take time to answer.

Some truths reveal themselves slowly.

And some discoveries arrive quietly when we least expect them.

But the journey is always worth taking. Because the answers you may be searching for are not waiting somewhere beyond you. They are waiting within you. Perhaps for the moment when you finally pause long enough to listen.

If these words ever find their way to someone reading them long after I have moved on from this space, I hope they carry a simple message forward.

You do not have to become someone else.

You only have to remember who you are.

Life is the whole.

Everything else lives inside it.

And when you return to yourself, you may discover something that was always true.

You were never lost.

You were simply waiting to remember and return.

-KAT

A Quiet Invitation to Remember

Many people spend their lives believing they are on a journey of becoming. The reflections within this book do not follow a traditional path of instruction. They follow a path of recognition.

Each chapter reflects a stage of a journey that unfolded slowly over time. Life's journey does not require becoming someone new. It requires honesty and stillness.

If you find yourself reading these pages during a season of reflection in your own life, I hope they offer something simple.

Not answers.

But recognition.

Recognition that the clarity you are looking for may already exist within you. Because the truth is this:

You do not have to become.

You only have to remember.

And remembering is the path that leads us home.

Karen Abbott Trimuel is a clarity coach, speaker, and guide who helps individuals reconnect with the truth of who they are beneath the expectations and roles that life often places upon them.

Her work centers on self-rediscovery, personal alignment, boundaries, and the wholeness that emerges when mind, body, and spirit begin moving together again.

Through workshops, coaching, and community gatherings, she has created spaces where people are invited to reflect honestly on their lives and rediscover the voice that often becomes quiet beneath the responsibilities of everyday living.

Karen is also the creator of the workbook *Unlocking the Answers to Who I Am*, a reflective guide that invites readers to explore the deeper questions that lead to self-awareness and inner clarity.

She is also the author of *Ladies Night Unmasked*, a fictional story about five friends navigating life, friendship, and personal truth, and *Check Your Assets & Know Your Value*, a woman's guide to becoming her authentic self.

Her journey – like the one shared in this book – is rooted in a simple realization:

The answers we search for are often waiting quietly within us.

When she is not writing or coaching, Karen enjoys spending time with her family, reflecting, engaging in meaningful conversations, and continuing to create spaces where others feel safe to remember who they are.

To learn more about her work, visit:
www.karenabbotttrimuel.com

www.ingramcontent.com/pod-product-compliance
Lightning Source LLC
Chambersburg PA
CBHW021340060726
47591CB00006B/2114